your **AVAILABLE**
P**OWER**

154650

P9-DTM-185

your AVAILABLE POWER

CHARLES SPURGEON

Whitaker House

All Scripture quotations are from the *King James Version* (KJV) of the Bible.

YOUR AVAILABLE POWER

ISBN: 0-88368-266-4
Printed in the United States of America
Copyright © 1996 by Whitaker House

Whitaker House
580 Pittsburgh Street
Springdale, PA 15144

No part of this book may be reproduced or transmitted in any form or by any means, electronic or mechanical, including photocopying, recording, or by any information storage and retrieval system, without permission in writing from the publisher.

1 2 3 4 5 6 7 8 9 10 11 / 05 04 03 02 01 00 99 98 97 96

48.4
93y

LIFE Pacific College
Alumni Library
1100 West Covina Blvd.
San Dimas, CA 91773

Contents

056010

Chapter One

On Speaking Well

May all the prayers you offer up be answered abundantly and speedily! May you plead with others in united prayer. The most memorable part of many meetings is the holy concert of believing prayer. I trust that you will grow fervent and powerful in intercession. On his knees, the believer is invincible.

I would like to discuss the topic of preaching. When I preach, I like to be able to speak well, having the best of speech well enlisted; but I desire to be absolutely in the Lord's hands in this matter as well as in every other. I would be willing to speak with stammering tongue if that would accomplish God's purpose more fully. I would even gladly lose all power of speech if, by being famished as to human words, the hearers might feed the better on that spiritual meat that is to be found alone in Christ, who is the incarnate Word of God.

I address the following to speakers. I am persuaded we should prepare ourselves with diligence, and we should try to do our very best in our great Master's service. I think I have read that when a handful of lion-like Greeks held the pass against the Persians, a spy came to see what they were doing. He went back and told the great king that they were poor creatures, for they were busy combing their hair. The despot saw things in a true light when he learned that a people who could style their hair before battle had set a great value on their heads and would not yield them to a coward's death.

If we are very careful to use our best language when proclaiming eternal truths, our opponents will infer that we are even more careful of the doctrines themselves. We must not be untidy soldiers when a great fight is before us, for that would look like despondency. Into the battle against false doctrine, worldliness, and sin, we advance without a fear about the ultimate outcome; therefore, our talk should not be that of ragged passion but of well-considered principle. It is not ours to be slovenly, for we look to be triumphant. Do your work well at this time so that all men may see that you are not going to be driven from it.

The Persian said, when on another occasion he saw a handful of warriors advancing, "That little handful of men! Surely, they cannot plan on fighting!" But someone who was standing there said, "Yes they do, for they have burnished their shields and brightened their armor."

Men mean business, count on it, when they are not to be hurried into disorder. It was a way among the Greeks, when they had a bloody day before them, to show the stern joy of warriors by being well adorned.

I think that when we have great work to do for Christ and mean to do it, we will not say the first thing that comes to the lip. If we speak for Jesus, we ought to speak at our best. Even then, men are not killed by the glitter of shields or by the smoothness of a warrior's hair, but a higher power is needed to cut through coats of mail.

To the God of armies I look up when I preach. May He defend the right! But with no careless step do I advance to the front to preach; neither does any doubt possess me. We are feeble, but the Lord our God is mighty. "The battle is the Lord's" (1 Sam. 17:47) rather than ours.

Only one fear is upon me to a certain degree. When I preach, I do not want my deep sense of responsibility to lessen my efficiency. A man might feel that he ought to do so well that, for that very reason, he might not do as well as he could have. An overpowering feeling of responsibility may breed paralysis.

I once recommended a young clerk to a bank, and his friends very properly gave him strict instructions to be very careful in his figures. This advice he heard times without end. He became so extremely careful that he grew nervous. Whereas he had been accurate before, his anxiety caused him to make blunder after blunder until he left his job.

It is possible to be so anxious about how and what you should speak that your manner grows constrained and you forget those very points that you meant to emphasize. We must prepare, but we must also trust in Him without whom nothing begins, continues, or ends right.

I have this comfort when I preach: even if I do not speak adequately on my theme, the topic itself will speak. There is something even in starting an appropriate subject. If a man speaks well on a subject that has no practical importance, it is better if he does not speak. As one of the ancients said, "It is idle to speak much to the point upon a matter which itself is not to the point."

Carve a cherry stone with the utmost skill, and at best it is but a cherry stone; while a diamond, if badly cut, is still a precious stone. If the matter is of great weight, even if the man cannot speak up to his theme, yet to call attention to it is no vain thing.

As a smith can teach his apprentice *while* making a horseshoe and *by* making a horseshoe, so we can make our own sermons examples of the doctrine they contain. (For example, if we preach that men should quote more from the Bible, we can quote more from the Bible as we preach.) We can practice while we preach if the Lord is with us.

A cooking instructor teaches his pupils by following his own recipes. He prepares a dish before his audience. While he describes the dishes and their preparation, he tastes the food himself, and his friends are refreshed also. He will impress them with his dainty dishes, even if he is not a man of eloquent speech. The man who feeds others is surer of success than he who only plays well upon an instrument and leaves with

12

his audience no memory but that of pleasant sound.

If the subjects that we bring before our people are in themselves good, they will make up for our want of skill in setting them forth. As long as the guests get the spiritual meat, the waiter at the table may be happy to be forgotten.

Chapter Two

Our Armory: The Bible

The subjects that I will now set forth ought to be considered, and they ought to be considered right now. I have chosen pressing truths, and if you will think them through for yourselves, you will not lose the time it takes to read this. With what inward fervor do I pray that you may be profited by the following meditation!

My topics have to do with our life-work, with the crusade against error and sin in which we are engaged. I hope that every one of you wears the red cross on his heart and is pledged to do and dare for Christ and for His Cross. I hope you will never be satisfied until Christ's foes are routed and Christ Himself is satisfied. Our fathers used to speak of "the cause of God and truth"; and it is for this that we bear arms, the few against the many, the feeble against the mighty. Oh, to be found good soldiers of Jesus Christ!

Three things are of the utmost importance just now; indeed, they always have stood and always will stand in the front rank. The first is *our armory,* which is the inspired Word. The second is *our army,* the church of the living God, called out by Himself, which we must lead under our Lord's command. The third is *our strength,* by which we wear the armor and wield the sword. The Holy Spirit is our power to be and to do, to suffer and to serve, to grow and to fight, to wrestle and to overcome. Our third theme is of utmost importance, and though we place it last, we rank it first.

We will begin with our armory. That armory is to me, at any rate—and I hope it is to each one of you—the Bible. To us,

Holy Scripture is as "the tower of David builded for an armoury, whereon there hang a thousand bucklers, all shields of mighty men" (Song 4:4). If we want weapons, we must come here for them, and here only. Whether we seek the sword of offense or the shield of defense, we must find it within the Volume of inspiration.

If others have any other storehouse, I confess at once that I have none. I have nothing else to preach when I am through with this Book. Indeed, I can have no wish to preach at all if I may not continue to expound the subjects that I find in these pages. What else is worth preaching? The truth of God is the only treasure for which we seek, and the Scripture is the only field in which we dig for it.

God's Word Is Our Foundation

We need nothing more than God has seen fit to reveal. Certain religious nomads are never at home until they are abroad; they crave for a something that I

think they will never find, either in
heaven above, or in the earth beneath,
or in the water under the earth, as long
as they are in their present mind. They
never rest, for they will have nothing to
do with an infallible revelation. Hence,
they are doomed to wander throughout
time and eternity and find no abiding
city.

For the moment they glory as if they
were satisfied with their latest new toy,
but in a few months it is sport to them
to break in pieces all the notions that
they formerly prepared with care and
paraded with delight. They go up a hill
only to come down again. Indeed, they
say that the pursuit of truth is better
than truth itself. They like fishing better
than the fish; I can see why, since their
fish are very small and very full of
bones.

These men are as great at destroying
their own theories as certain beggars are
at tearing up their clothes. They begin
all over again times without number;
their house is always having its foundation dug out. They should be good at

beginnings, for they have always been beginning since we have known them. They are as the "rolling thing before the whirlwind" (Isa. 17:13) or "like the troubled sea, when it cannot rest, whose waters cast up mire and dirt" (Isa. 57:20). Although their cloud is not that cloud which was a token of the divine presence (see Exodus 13:21), yet it is always moving before them; their tents are hardly pitched before it is time for the stakes to be pulled up again.

These men are not even seeking certainty; their heaven lies in shunning all fixed truth and following every will-o'-the-wisp of speculation. They are "ever learning, and never able to come to the knowledge of the truth" (2 Tim. 3:7).

As for us, we cast anchor in the haven of the Word of God. Here is our peace, our strength, our life, our motive, our hope, our happiness. God's Word is our ultimatum. Here we have it. Our understanding cries, "I have found it." Our conscience asserts that here is the truth. Our heart finds here a support to which all her affections can cling. In God's Word we rest content.

God's Word Is All-Sufficient

If the revelation of God were not enough for our faith, what could we add to it? Who can answer this question? What would any man propose to add to the sacred Word? A moment's thought would lead us to mock with derision the most attractive words of men if it were proposed to add them to the Word of God. The fabric would not be of one piece. Would you add rags to a royal garment? (See Luke 5:36.) Would you pile the filth of the streets in a king's treasury? Would you join the pebbles of the seashore to the diamonds of Golconda?

Anything more than what the Word of God sets before us, for us to believe and to preach as the life of men, seems utterly absurd to us; yet we confront a generation of preachers who are always wanting to discover a new motive power and a new gospel for their churches. The bedspread on their bed does not seem to be long enough, and they would gladly borrow a yard or two of fabric from the Unitarian, the agnostic, or even the atheist.

Well, if there is any spiritual force or heavenward power to be found beyond that reported of in this Book, I think we can do without it; indeed, it must be such a sham that we are better without it. The Scriptures in their own sphere are like God in the universe, all-sufficient. In them is revealed all the light and power the mind of man can need in spiritual things. We hear of another motive power beyond that which lies in the Scriptures, but we believe such a force to be a pretentious nothing.

A train is off the tracks or otherwise unable to proceed, and a breakdown crew has arrived. Engines are brought to move the huge train. At first there seems to be no stir; the engine power is not enough. Listen! A small boy has the answer. He cries, "Father, if they do not have enough power, I will lend them my rocking horse to help them."

We have had the offers of a considerable number of rocking horses of late. They have not accomplished much that I can see, but they promised much. I fear their effect has been for evil rather than good; they have moved the people to derision, and they have driven them out of the places of worship that once they were glad to crowd. The new toys have been exhibited, and the people, after seeing them a little, have moved on to other toyshops. These fine, new nothings have done no good, and they never will do any good while the world stands. The Word of God is quite sufficient to interest and bless the souls of men throughout all time, but novelties soon fail.

"Surely," cries one, "we must add our own thoughts to God's Word." My fellow believer, think by all means, but the thoughts of God are better than yours. You may shed fine thoughts, as trees in autumn cast their leaves; however, there is One who knows more about your thoughts than you do, and He thinks little of them. Is it not written, "The LORD knoweth the thoughts of man, that they are vanity" (Ps. 94:11)?

To liken our thoughts to the great thoughts of God would be a gross absurdity. Would you bring your candle to show the sun? Your nothingness to replenish the eternal all? It is better to be silent before the Lord than to dream of supplementing what He has spoken. The Word of the Lord is to the conceptions of men as a garden to a wilderness. Keep within the covers of the Sacred Book, and you are in the land that flows with milk and honey; why seek to add to it the desert sands?

Try not to discard anything from the Sacred Volume. If you find it there, there let it stand. Let it be preached according to the analogy and proportion of faith. That which is worthy of God's revealing is worthy of our preaching, and that is much too little for me to claim for it. "By every word that proceedeth out of the mouth of the LORD doth man live"

23

(Deut. 8:3). "Every word of God is pure: he is a shield unto them that put their trust in him" (Prov. 30:5).

Let every revealed truth be brought forth in its own season. There is no need to go elsewhere for a subject to preach. With such infinity before you, there can be no need that you should do so; with such glorious truth to preach, it will be unjustifiable wickedness if you do.

God's Word Has Been Tested

The adaptation of all this provision for our warfare we have already tested. The weapons of our armory are the very best, for we have put them to the test and have found them so. Some of you that are younger have only tested the Scripture a little so far; but others of us, who are now getting gray, can assure you that we have tried the Word "as silver [is] tried in a furnace of earth" (Ps. 12:6). It has stood every test, even unto seventy times seven.

The sacred Word has endured more criticism than the best accepted form of philosophy or science, and it has survived every ordeal. As one theologian said, "After its present assailants are all dead, their funeral sermons will be preached from this Book—not one verse omitted—from the first page of Genesis to the last page of Revelation."

Some of us have lived for many years, in daily conflict, perpetually putting to the test the Word of God. We can honestly give you this assurance: it is equal to every emergency. After using this sword of two edges on coats of mail and bucklers of brass, we find no notch in its edge. It is neither broken nor blunted in the fight. It would split the Devil himself from the top of his head to the sole of his foot, and yet it would show no sign of failure whatsoever.

Today it is still the selfsame mighty Word of God that it was in the hands of our Lord Jesus. How it strengthens us when we remember the many conquests of souls that we have achieved through the sword of the Spirit!

Have you known or heard of such a thing as conversion brought about by any other doctrine than that which is in the Word? I would like to have a catalog of conversions brought about by modern theology. I would subscribe for a copy of such a work. I will not say what I might do with it after I had read it, but I would, at least, increase its sale by one copy just to see what progressive divinity pretends to have done.

Conversions through the doctrine of universal restitution! Conversions through the doctrine of doubtful inspiration! Conversions to the love of God and faith in Christ by hearing that the death of the Savior was only the consummation of a grand example but not a substitutionary sacrifice! Conversions by a gospel out of which all the Gospel has been drained! They say, "Wonders will never cease," but such wonders will never begin.

Let them report changes of heart brought about this way and give us an opportunity of testing them; then, perhaps, we may consider whether it is worth our while to leave that Word which we have tried in hundreds and thousands of cases and have always found effective for salvation. We know why they sneer at conversions. These are grapes that such foxes cannot reach, and therefore they are sour.

Because we believe in the new birth and expect to see it in thousands of cases, we will adhere to that Word of truth by which the Holy Spirit works regeneration. In a word, we will keep to the old weapon of the sword of the Spirit in our warfare until we can find a better. At present, our verdict is, "There is none like that; give it me" (1 Sam. 21:9).

How often we have seen the Word made effective for consolation! It is, as one brother expressed it in prayer, a difficult thing to deal with broken hearts. What a fool I have felt myself to be when trying to bring forth a prisoner out of Giant Despair's castle! How hard it is to persuade despondency to hope! How I have tried to trap my game by every art known to me, but when almost in my grasp, the creature has burrowed another hole! I had dug him out of twenty already and then have had to begin again. The convicted sinner uses all kinds of arguments to prove that he cannot be saved. The inventions of despair are as many as the devices of self-confidence. There is no letting light into the dark cellar of doubt except through the window of the Word of God.

Within the Scripture there is a balm for every wound, a salve for every sore. Oh, the wondrous power in the Scripture to create a soul of hope within the ribs of despair and to bring eternal light into the darkness that has made a long midnight in the inmost soul! Often have we tried the Word of the Lord as "the cup of consolation" (Jer. 16:7), and it has never failed to cheer the despondent. We know what we say, for we have witnessed the blessed facts: the Scriptures of truth, applied by the Holy Spirit, have brought peace and joy to those who "sat in darkness" and "in the region and shadow of death" (Matt. 4:16).

We have also observed the excellence of the Word in the edification of believers and in the production of righteousness, holiness, and usefulness. We are always being told these days of the "ethical" side of the Gospel. I pity those to whom this is a novelty. Have they not discovered this before? We have always been dealing with the ethical side of the Gospel; indeed, we find it ethical all over. There is no true doctrine that has not been fruitful in good works. Payson wisely said, "If there is one fact, one doctrine, or promise in the Bible that has produced no practical effect on your temper or conduct, be assured that you do not truly believe it."

All scriptural teaching has its practical purpose and its practical result. What we have to say, not as a matter of discovery but as a matter of plain common sense, is this: if we have had fewer fruits than we want with the tree, we suspect that there will be no fruit at all when the tree is gone and the roots dug up. The very root of holiness lies in the Gospel of our Lord Jesus Christ. If this is removed with a view to more fruitfulness, the most astounding folly will have been committed.

We have seen a fine morality, a stern integrity, a delicate purity, and—what is more—a devout holiness produced by the doctrines of grace. We see consecration in life; we see calm resignation in the hour of suffering; we see joyful confidence in the time of death. Moreover, these are not what we see in a few instances, but these are the general outcomes of intelligent faith in the teachings of Scripture. We have even been amazed at the sacred result of the old Gospel. Though we are accustomed to seeing it often, it never loses its charm. We have seen poor men and women yielding themselves to Christ and living for Him in a way that has made our hearts bow in adoration of the God of grace. We have said, "This must be a true Gospel that can produce such lives as these."

If we have not talked as much about ethics as some have done, we remember an old saying of the country folk: "Go to such and such a place to hear about good works, but go to another place to see them." Much talk, little work. Great cry is the token of little wool. Some have preached good works until there has scarcely been a decent person left in the parish, while others have preached free grace and dying love in such a way that sinners have become saints, and saints have been as boughs loaded down with fruit to the praise and glory of God. Having seen the harvest that springs from our seed, we are not going to change it at the dictates of this whimsical age.

We have especially seen and tested the efficacy of the Word of God when we have been by the sickbed. I was, but a few days ago, by the side of one of our elders, who appeared to be dying; and it was like heaven below to converse with him. I never saw so much joy at a wedding as I saw in that quiet chamber. He hoped soon to be with Jesus, and he was joyful in the prospect. He said, "I have no doubt, no cloud, no trouble, no want; no, I do not even have a wish. The doctrine you have taught has served me to live by, and now it serves me to die by. I am resting upon the precious blood of Christ, and it is a firm foundation." And he added, "How silly all those articles against the Gospel now appear to me! I have read some of them, and I have noted the attacks on the old faith, but they seem quite absurd to me now that I lie on the verge of eternity. What could the new doctrine do for me now?"

I came from my visit greatly strengthened and gladdened by the good man's testimony, and I was personally comforted even more because it was the Word that I myself had constantly preached that had been such a blessing to my friend. If God had so allowed it through so poor an instrument, I felt that the Word itself must be good indeed.

I am never as happy amid all the shouts of youthful merriment as on the day when I hear the dying testimony of one who is resting on the everlasting Gospel of the grace of God. The ultimate issue, as seen upon a deathbed, is a true test, as well as an inevitable one. If a man preaches that which will enable men to face death without fear, he will preach nothing but the old Gospel.

We will array ourselves in that which God has supplied us in the armory of inspired Scripture. Every weapon in it has been tried and proved in many ways, and never has any part of our armor failed us.

Chapter Three

The Power of the Bible

We will evermore keep to the Word of God because we have had experience of its power within ourselves. It has not been so long ago that you will have forgotten how, like a hammer, the Word of God broke your flinty heart and brought down your stubborn will. By the Word of the Lord you were brought to the cross and comforted by the atonement. That Word breathed a new life into you; and when, for the first time, you knew yourself to be a child of God, you felt the ennobling power of the Gospel received by faith.

The Holy Spirit worked your salvation through the Holy Scriptures.

You trace your conversion, I am sure, to the Word of the Lord, for this alone is "perfect, converting the soul" (Ps. 19:7). Whoever may have been the man who spoke it or whatever may have been the book in which you read it, it was not man's word, nor man's thought upon God's Word, but the Word itself that made you know salvation in the Lord Jesus. It was neither human reasoning nor the force of eloquence nor the power of moral persuasion that brought you to Christ. It was the omnipotence of the Spirit, applying the Word itself, that gave you rest and peace and joy through believing. We are ourselves trophies of the power of the sword of the Spirit; He leads us in triumph in every place, the willing captives of His grace. Let no man marvel that we keep close to it.

How many times since conversion has Holy Scripture been everything to you? You have your fainting fits, I suppose. Have you not been revived by the precious promise of the Faithful One? A passage of Scripture laid home to the heart speedily quickens the feeble heart into mighty action. Men speak of waters that revive the spirits and tonics that brace the constitution, but the Word of God has been more than this to us, times beyond count. Amid temptations sharp and strong, and trials fierce and bitter, the Word of the Lord has preserved us. Amid discouragements that dampened our hopes and disappointments that wounded our hearts, we have felt ourselves strong to do and bear, for the assurances of help that we find in our Bibles have brought us a secret, unconquerable energy.

We have experienced the elevation that the Word of God can give—uplifting towards God and heaven. If you start to study books contrary to the inspired volume, are you not conscious of slipping downwards? I have known some to whom such reading has been as a foul-smelling vapor surrounding them with the death-damp. Yes, and I may add that to forego your Bible reading for the perusal even of good books would soon bring a conscious descending of the soul. Have you not found that even good books may be to you as a plain to look down upon, rather than as a summit to which to aspire? You have come up to their level long ago and get no higher by reading them; it is idle to spend precious time on them.

Was it ever so with you and the Book of God? Did you ever rise above its simplest teaching and feel that it tended to draw you downward? Never! In proportion as your mind becomes saturated with Holy Scripture, you are conscious of being lifted right up and carried aloft as on eagles' wings.

You seldom finish a solitary Bible reading without feeling that you have drawn near to God. I say a solitary one; for when reading with others, the danger is that stale comments may be flies in the pot of ointment. The prayerful study of the Word is not only a means of instruction, but it is also an act of devotion wherein the transforming power of grace is often exercised, changing us into the image of Him of whom the Word is a mirror. Is there anything, after all, like the Word of God when the open book finds open hearts?

When I read the lives of such men as Baxter, Brainerd, McCheyne, and many others, why, I feel like one who has bathed himself in some cool brook after having gone on a journey through a dark country, which left him dusty and depressed. This result comes from the fact that such men embodied Scripture in their lives and illustrated it in their experience. The "washing of water by the word" (Eph. 5:26) is what they had and what we need. We must get it where they found it.

To see the effects of the truth of God in the lives of holy men is confirmatory to faith and stimulating to holy aspiration. Other influences do not help us to such a sublime ideal of consecration. If you read the Babylonian books of the present day, you will catch their spirit; and it is a foreign one, which will draw you aside from the Lord your God. You may also get great harm from theologians in whom there is much pretense of the Jerusalem dialect, but their speech is half of Ashdod (see Nehemiah 13:24); these will confuse your mind and defile your faith.

It may happen that a book that is on the whole excellent, which has a little taint about it, may do you more mischief than a thoroughly bad one. Be careful, for works of this kind come forth from the press like clouds of locusts. Scarcely can you find in these days a book that is quite free from the modern leaven, and the least particle of it ferments until it produces the wildest error. In reading books of the new order, though no palpable falsehood may appear, you are conscious of a twist being given you and of a sinking in the tone of your spirit; therefore, be on your guard.

However, with your Bible you may always feel at ease; there every breath from every quarter brings life and health (Prov. 4:22). If you keep close to the inspired book, you can suffer no harm; rather you are at the fountainhead of all moral and spiritual good.

This is fit food for men of God; this is the bread that nourishes the highest life.

God's Word Is Inexhaustible

After preaching the Gospel for forty years and after printing the sermons I have preached for more than thirty-six years, reaching now to the number of 2,200 in weekly succession, I am fairly entitled to speak about the fullness and richness of the Bible as a preacher's book. It is inexhaustible. No question about freshness will arise if we keep closely to the text of the Sacred Volume. There can be no difficulty in finding themes totally distinct from those that have been preached before; the variety is as infinite as the fullness.

A long life will only suffice us to skirt the shores of this great continent of light. In the forty years of my own ministry, I have only touched the hem of the garment of divine truth; but what virtue has flowed out of it! The

Word is like its Author—infinite, immeasurable, without end.

If you were ordained to be a preacher, throughout eternity you would have before you a theme equal to everlasting demands. Fellow believers, will we each have a pulpit somewhere amid the spheres? Will we have a parish of millions of miles? Will we have voices so strong they will reach attentive constellations? Will we be witnesses for the Lord of grace to myriads of worlds, which will be wonder-struck when they hear of the incarnate God? Will we be surrounded by pure intelligences inquiring and searching into the mystery of God manifest in the flesh? Will the unfallen worlds desire to be instructed in the glorious Gospel of the blessed God? And will each one of us have his own tale to tell of his experience of infinite love?

I think so, since the Lord has saved us "to the intent that now unto the principalities and powers in heavenly places might be known by the church the manifold wisdom of God" (Eph. 3:10). If such is the case, our Bibles will suffice for ages to come for new themes every morning and for fresh songs and discourses world without end.

We are resolved, then, since we have this arsenal supplied for us by the Lord and since we want no other, to use the Word of God only and to use it with greater energy. We are resolved—and I hope that you will agree also—to know the Bible better. Do we know the Sacred Volume half as well as we should know it? Do we know the Word of God as well as many a critic knows his favorite classic? Is it not possible that we still find passages of Scripture that are new to us? Should it be so? Is there any part of what the Lord has written that you have never read?

I was struck with my brother Archibald Brown's observation that unless he read the Scriptures through from end to end there might be inspired teachings that he had never discovered. So he resolved to read the books in their order; and, having done so once, he continued the habit. Have we omitted to do this? Let us begin at once.

I love to see how readily certain believers find an appropriate passage, then quote a related verse, and top it all off with a third. They seem to know exactly the passage that strikes the nail on the head. They have their Bibles not only in their hearts but at their fingers' ends.

This is a most valuable attainment for a minister. A good textuary is a good theologian. Certain others, whom I esteem for other things, are yet weak on this point and seldom quote a text of Scripture correctly; indeed, their alterations jar on the ear of the Bible reader. It is sadly common among ministers to add a word or subtract a word from the passage, or in some way to debase the language of Sacred Writ. How often I have heard believers speak about making "your calling and salvation" sure! Possibly they hardly enjoyed so much as we do the Calvinistic word "election" (2 Pet. 1:10), and therefore they allowed it to disappear. Others quote half a text and therefore miss the meaning or even contradict it.

44

Our reverence for the great Author of Scripture should forbid all mauling of His words. No alteration of Scripture can by any possibility be an improvement. Believers in verbal inspiration should be studiously careful to be verbally correct. The gentlemen who see errors in Scripture may think themselves competent to amend the language of the Lord of Hosts, but we who believe God and accept the very words He uses may not make so presumptuous an attempt. Let us quote the words as they stand in the best possible translation, and it will be better still if we know the original and can tell if our version fails to give the sense.

How much mischief may arise out of an accidental alteration of the Word! Blessed are they who are in accord with the divine teaching and receive its true meaning as the Holy Spirit teaches them! Oh, that we might know the Spirit of Holy Scripture thoroughly, drinking it in until we are saturated with it! This is the blessing that we resolve to obtain.

Believe It

By God's grace, we purpose to believe the Word of God more intensely. There is believing, and *believing*. You believe in all your fellow Christians; but in some of them you have a conscious, practical confidence, since in your hour of trouble they have come to your rescue and proved themselves brothers "born for adversity" (Prov. 17:17). You confide in these with absolute certainty because you have personally tried them. Your faith was faith before, but now it is a higher, firmer, and more assured confidence.

Believe in the Sacred Volume up to the hilt. Believe it right through; believe it thoroughly; believe it with the whole strength of your being. Let the truths of Scripture become the chief factors in your life, the chief operative forces of your action. Let the great transactions of the gospel story be as real and practical to you as any fact that meets you in the domestic circle or in the outside world. Let them be as vividly true to you as your own ever present body with its aches and pains, its appetites and joys.

If we can get out of the realm of fiction and fancy into the world of fact, we will have struck a vein of power that will yield us a countless treasure of strength. Thus, to become "mighty in the Scriptures" (Acts 18:24) will be to become "mighty through God" (2 Cor. 10:4).

Quote It

We should resolve also that we will quote more of Holy Scriptures. Sermons should be full of the Bible—sweetened, strengthened, sanctified with Bible essence. The kind of teachings that people need to hear are outgrowths of Scripture. If they do not love to hear them, that is all the more reason why they should be preached to them. The Gospel has the singular faculty of creating a taste for itself. Bible hearers, when they hear indeed, come to be Bible lovers.

The mere stringing together of texts is a poor way of making sermons;

however, some have tried it, and I do not doubt that God has blessed them since they did their best. It is far better to string texts together than to pour out one's own poor thoughts in a washy flood. There will at least be something to be thought of and remembered if the Holy Word is quoted, and in the other case there may be nothing whatsoever.

Texts of Scripture need not, however, be strung together; they may be fitly brought in to give edge and focus to a point. They will be the force of the sermon. Our own words are mere paper pellets compared with the rifle shot of the Word. The Scripture is the conclusion of the whole matter. There is no arguing after we find that "it is written" (Matt. 4:4, 7, 10). To a large extent, the debate in the hearts and consciences of hearers is finished when they know the Lord has spoken. "Thus saith the Lord" is the end of discussion to Christian minds, and even the ungodly cannot resist Scripture without resisting the Spirit who wrote it. In order that we may speak convincingly, we will speak scripturally.

Preach It

We are further resolved that we will preach nothing but the Word of God. The alienation of the masses from hearing the Gospel is largely due to the sad fact that it is not always the Gospel that they hear if they go to some places of worship, and all else falls short of what their souls need.

Have you ever heard of a king who made a series of great feasts and invited many, week after week? He had a number of servants who were appointed to wait at his table, and these went out on the appointed days and spoke with the people. But, somehow, after a while the bulk of the people did not come to the feasts. They came in decreasing number, but the great mass of the citizens turned their backs on the banquets.

The king made inquiry. He found that the food provided did not seem to satisfy the men who came to the banquets, and so they came no more. He determined to examine the tables and the food himself. He saw much finery and many pieces of display that never came out of his storehouses. He looked at the food, and he said, "But how can this be? These dishes, how did they get here? I did not provide these. My oxen and my fatlings were killed, yet we do not have here the flesh of fed beasts but hard meat from cattle lean and starved. Bones are here, but where is the fat and the marrow? The bread also is coarse, whereas mine was made of the finest of the wheat. The wine is mixed with water, and the water is not from a pure well."

One of those who stood by answered and said, "O king, we thought that the people would be tired of marrow and fatness, and so we gave them bone and gristle to try their teeth on. We thought also that they would be weary of the best white bread, and so we baked a little at our own homes, in which the bran and husks were allowed to remain. It is the opinion of the learned that our provision is more suitable for these times than that which your majesty prescribed so long ago. As for the wines, men do not like them these days; and a liquid so transparent as pure water is too light a drink for men who are used to drinking of the river of Egypt, which has a taste of mud in it from the Mountains of the Moon." Then the king knew why the people did not come to the feast.

Going to the house of God has become distasteful to a great many of the population. Does the reason lie in this direction? I believe it does. Have our Lord's servants been chopping up their own odds and ends and tainted bits to make with them a stew for the millions, and do the millions therefore turn away? Listen to the rest of my parable.

"Clear the tables!" cried the king in indignation. "Cast that rubbish to the dogs. Bring in the sirloins of beef; set forth my royal provisions. Remove those whatnots from the hall and that adulterated bread from the table, and cast out the water of the muddy river."

They did so; and if my parable is right, very soon there was a rumor throughout the streets that truly royal dainties were to be had. The people thronged the palace, and the king's name became exceeding great throughout the land. Let us try the plan. Maybe we will soon rejoice to see our Master's banquet furnished with guests.

Chapter Four

The Inspiration of the Bible

We are resolved to use more fully than ever what God has provided for us in the Bible, for we are sure of its inspiration. Let me express that again: *We are sure of its inspiration.*

You will notice that attacks are frequently made against verbal inspiration. This form of attack is a mere pretext. Verbal inspiration is the form of the assault, but the attack is really aimed at inspiration itself. You will not read far in an essay before you will find that the gentleman who started with contesting a theory of inspiration that we never held winds up by showing his hand, and that hand wages war with inspiration itself. There is the true point.

We care little for any theory of inspiration; in fact, we have none. To us the complete verbal inspiration of Holy Scripture is fact and not hypothesis. It is a pity to theorize on a subject that is deeply mysterious and makes a demand on faith rather than fancy. Believe in the inspiration of Scripture, and believe it in the most intense sense. You will not believe in a truer and fuller inspiration than really exists. No one is likely to err in that direction, even if error would be possible. If you adopt theories that pare off a portion here and deny authority to a passage there, you will at last have no inspiration left worthy of the name.

If this book is not infallible, where will we find infallibility? We have given up the pope, for he has blundered often and terribly; but we will not set up instead of him a horde of little popelings fresh from college. Are these correctors of Scripture infallible? Is it certain that our Bibles are not right but that the critics must be right? The old silver is to be depreciated; but the German silver, which is put in its place, is to be taken at the value of gold. Youths fresh from reading the last new novel correct the notions of their fathers, who were men of weight and character. Doctrines that produced the godliest generation that ever lived on the face of the earth are scoffed at as sheer folly.

Nothing is so obnoxious to these creatures as that which smells of Puritanism. Every little man's nose goes up celestially at the very sound of the word "Puritan." If the Puritans were here again, they would not dare to treat them thus cavalierly. If Puritans did fight, they were soon known as Ironsides, and their leader could hardly be called a fool, even by those who stigmatized him as a tyrant. Cromwell and they that were with him were not all weak-minded persons, surely? Strange that these are extolled to the skies by the very men who deride their true successors, believers in the same faith.

But where can infallibility be found? "The depth saith, It is not in me" (Job 28:14); yet those who have no depth at all would have us imagine that it is in them, or else by perpetual change they hope to hit upon it. Are we to believe that infallibility is with learned men? Now, Farmer Smith, when you have read your Bible and have enjoyed its precious promises, you will have to go down the street tomorrow morning to ask the scholarly man at the parsonage whether this portion of the Scripture belongs to the inspired part of the Word or whether it is of dubious authority. It will be well for you to know whether it was written by *the* Isaiah or whether it was by the second of the "two Obadi-ahs."

All possibility of certainty is transferred from spiritual men to a class of persons whose scholarship is pretentious but who do not even pretend to spirituality. We will gradually be so doubtful and criticized that only a few of the most profound will know what is Bible and what is not, and they will dictate to all the rest of us. I have no more faith in their mercy than in their accuracy; they will rob us of all that we hold most dear and glory in the cruel deed.

This same reign of terror we will not endure, for we still believe that God reveals Himself rather to babes than to the wise and prudent (Matt. 11:25). Furthermore, we are fully assured that our own old English version of the Scriptures is sufficient for plain men for all purposes of life, salvation, and godliness. We do not despise learning, but we will never say of culture or criticism, "These be thy gods, O Israel" (Exod. 32:4)!

Do you see why men would lower the degree of inspiration in Holy Writ and would gladly reduce it to an infinitesimal quantity? It is because the truth of God is to be supplanted.

Do you ever go to a store in the evening to buy certain products which are judged by their color and texture and need to be examined in good lighting? If, after you go into the store, the salesman first lowers the lights and then commences to show you his products, your suspicion is aroused, and you conclude that he will try to palm off an inferior article.

I more than suspect this to be the little game of the inspiration-depreciators. Whenever a man begins to lower your view of inspiration, it is because he has a trick to play that is not easily performed in the light. He would hold a séance of evil spirits, and therefore he cries, "Let the lights be lowered."

We are willing to ascribe to the Word of God all the inspiration that can possibly be ascribed to it; and we say boldly that if our preaching is "not according to this Word, it is because there is no light in [it]" (Isa. 8:20). We are willing to be tried and tested by the Word in every way. We count those who search the Scriptures daily to see whether these things are so to be the noblest of our hearers. (See Acts 17:11.) But to those who belittle inspiration we will give "place by subjection, no, not for an hour" (Gal. 2:5).

Do I hear someone say, "But still you must submit to the conclusions of science"? No one is more ready than we are to accept the evident facts of science. But what do you mean by science? Is the thing called "science" infallible? Is it not "science falsely so called" (1 Tim. 6:20)? The history of human ignorance that calls itself "philosophy" is absolutely identical with the history of fools, except where it diverges into madness. If another Erasmus were to arise and write the history of folly, he would have to give several chapters to philosophy and science, and those chapters would be more telling than any others.

I myself would not dare to say that philosophers and scientists are generally fools, but I would give them liberty to speak of one another. At the close I would then say, "Gentlemen, you are less complimentary to each other than I would have been." I would let the wise of each generation speak of the generation that went before it, or nowadays each half of a generation might deal with the previous half generation. There is little of theory in science today that will survive twenty years, and only a little more that will see the first day of the twentieth century.

We travel now at so rapid a rate that we rush by sets of scientific hypotheses as quickly as we pass fence posts when riding in an express train. All that we are certain of today is this: what the learned were sure of a few years ago is now thrown into the limbo of discarded errors.

I believe in science but not in what is called "science." No proven fact in nature is opposed to revelation. The pretty speculations of the pretentious we cannot reconcile with the Bible, and we would not if we could. I feel like the man who said, "I can understand in some degree how these great men have found out the weight of the stars and their distances from one another, and even how, by the spectroscope, they have discovered the materials of which they are composed. But," said he, "I cannot guess how they found out their names."

That is right. The fanciful part of science, so dear to many, is what we do not accept. That is the important part of science to many—that part which is a mere guess, for which the guessers fight tooth and nail. The mythology of science is as false as the mythology of the heathen, but this is the thing that is made into a god. I say again, science is never in conflict with the truths of Holy Scripture as far as its facts are concerned; but the hurried deductions drawn from those facts and the inventions classed as facts are opposed to Scripture, and necessarily so, because falsehood agrees not with truth.

Two sorts of people have done great mischief, and yet neither of them are worth being considered as judges in the matter; they are both of them disqualified. It is essential that an umpire should know both sides of a question, and neither of these is thus instructed. The first is the irreligious scientist. What does he know about religion? What can he know? He is not eligible to answer the question, Does science agree with religion? Obviously, he who would answer this query must know both of the two things in the question.

The second is a better man, but he is capable of still more mischief. I am talking about the unscientific Christian who will trouble his head about reconciling the Bible with science. He had better leave it alone and not begin his tinkering trade. The mistake made by such men has been that, in trying to solve a difficulty, they have either twisted the Bible or contorted science. Their solutions are soon proven to be erroneous, and then we hear the cry that Scripture has been defeated. Not at all, not at all. It is only a vain gloss upon it that has been removed.

Here is a good brother who writes a tremendous book to prove that the six days of Creation represent six great geological periods. He shows how the geological strata and the organisms thereof follow the order of the Genesis story of Creation very closely. It may be so, or it may not be so; but if anybody should soon show that the strata do not lie in any such order, what would be my reply? I would say that the Bible never taught that they did.

The Bible says, "In the beginning God created the heaven and the earth" (Gen. 1:1). That leaves any length of time for your fire ages and your ice periods and all that before the establishment of the present age of man. Then we reach the six days in which the Lord made the heavens and the earth and rested on the seventh day. There is nothing said about long ages of time; on the contrary, "the evening and the morning were the first day" (Gen. 1:5), "the evening and the morning were the second day" (Gen. 1:8), and so on.

I am not proposing any theory, but I simply say that if our friend's great book is all fudge, the Bible is not responsible for it. It is true that his theory has an appearance of support from the parallelism that he points out between the organic life of the ages and that of the seven days, but this may be accounted for from the fact that God usually follows a certain order whether he works in long periods or in short ones. I do not know and I do not care much about the question; but I want to say that if you tear down an explanation, you must not imagine that you have damaged the scriptural truth that seemed to require the explanation. You have only burned the wooden palisades with which well-meaning men thought to protect an impregnable fort which needed no such defense.

For the most part, we had better leave a difficulty where it is rather than make another difficulty by our theory. Why make a second hole in the kettle to mend the first, especially when the first hole is not there at all and needs no mending? Believe everything in science that is proved; it will not be much. You need not fear that your faith will be overburdened. Then believe everything that is clearly in the Word of God, whether it is proved by outside evidence or not. No proof is needed when God speaks. If He has said it, this is evidence enough.

But we are told that we ought to give up a part of our old-fashioned theology to save the rest. We are in a carriage traveling over the steppes of Russia. The horses are being driven furiously, but the wolves are close behind us! There they are! Can you not see their eyes of fire? We are in dire danger. What must we do?

It is proposed that we throw out a child or two. By the time they have eaten the baby, we will have made a little headway; but should they again overtake us, what then? Why, brave man, throw out your wife! "All that a man hath will he give for his life" (Job 2:4).

Give up nearly every truth in the hope of saving one. Throw out inspiration, and let the critics devour it. Throw out election and all the old Calvinism; here will be a dainty feast for the wolves, and the gentlemen who give us the sage advice will be glad to see the doctrines of grace torn limb from limb. Throw out natural depravity, eternal punishment, and the efficacy of prayer. We have lightened the carriage wonderfully. Now for another heave-ho. Sacrifice the great sacrifice! Get rid of the atonement!

Beloved, this advice is villainous and murderous; we will escape these wolves with everything, or we will be lost with everything. It will be "the truth, the whole truth, and nothing but the truth," or none at all. We will never attempt to save half the truth by casting any part of it away. The sage advice that has been given to us involves treason to God and disappointment to ourselves. We will stand by all or none. We will have a whole Bible or no Bible.

We are told that if we give up something, the adversaries will also give up something; but we do not care what they will do, for we are not in the least afraid of them. They are not the imperial conquerors they think themselves. We ask no quarter from their insignificance. We are of the mind of the warrior who was offered presents to buy him off. He was told that if he accepted so much gold or territory, he could return home in triumph and glory in his easy gain. But he said, "The Greeks put no value on concessions. They find their glory not in presents, but in spoils."

With the sword of the Spirit we will maintain the whole truth as ours, and we will not accept a part of it as a grant from the enemies of God. The truth of God we will maintain as the truth of God, and we will not retain it because the philosophic mind consents to our doing so. If scientists agree to our believing a part of the Bible, we thank them for nothing; we believe it whether we have their permission or not. Their assent is of no more consequence to our faith than the consent of a Frenchman to the Englishman's holding London, or the consent of the mole to the eagle's sight. God being with us, we will not cease from this glorying, but we will hold fast to the whole of revealed truth, even to the end.

No Additions or Subtractions

But now, while keeping to this first part of my theme, perhaps for too long, I say to you that, believing this, we accept the obligation to preach everything that we see to be in the Word of God, as far as we see it. We would not willfully leave out any portion of the whole revelation of God, but we long to be able to say at the last, "[We] have not shunned to declare unto you all the counsel of God" (Acts 20:27). What mischief may come of leaving out any portion of the truth or putting in an alien element!

All good men will not agree with me when I say that the addition of infant baptism to the Word of God—for it certainly is not there—is filled with mischief. Baptismal regeneration rides in upon the shoulders of infant baptism. But I speak now what I know. I have received letters from missionaries—not Baptists, but Wesleyans and Congregationalists—who have said to me, "Since we have been here," (I will not mention the localities lest I get the good men into trouble), "we find a class of persons who are the children of former converts and who have been baptized and are therefore called Christians, but they are not one whit better than the heathen around them. They seem to think that they are Christians because of their baptism;

and, at the same time, being thought Christians by the heathen, their evil lives are a perpetual scandal and a dreadful stumbling block." This is, no doubt, a problem in many cases.

I only use this fact as an illustration. But suppose it to be either some other error invented or some great truth neglected, evil will come of it. In the case of the terrible truths known by us as "the terrors of the Lord," their omission is producing the saddest results. A good man, whom we do not accept as teaching exactly the truth upon this solemn matter, has, nevertheless, most faithfully written again and again to the papers to say that the great weakness of the modern pulpit is that it ignores the justice of God and the punishment of sin. His witness is true, and the evil that he indicates is incalculably great. You cannot leave out that part of the truth that is dark and solemn without weakening the force of all the other truths you preach. You are taking the truths that concern salvation from the wrath to come, and you are robbing them of their brightness and their urgent importance.

We must leave out nothing. We must be bold enough to preach unpalatable and unpopular truth. The evil that we may do by adding to or taking from the Word of the Lord may not happen in our own days; but if it should come to ripeness in another generation, we will be equally guilty. I have no doubt that the omission of certain truths by the earlier churches led afterwards to serious error. Certain additions in the form of rites and ceremonies, which appeared innocent enough in themselves, led to ritualism and afterwards to the great apostasy of Romanism!

We must be very careful. We must not go an inch beyond the line of Scripture or stay an inch on this side of it. We must keep to the straight line of the Word of God, as far as the Holy Spirit has taught us, and hold back nothing that He has revealed. We must not be so bold as to abolish the two ordinances that the Lord Jesus has ordained, though some have ventured upon that gross presumption; neither should we exaggerate those ordinances into inevitable channels of grace, as others have superstitiously done. We must keep to the revelation of the Spirit. We will have to give an account, and that account will not be with joy if we have played falsely with God's truth.

Remember the story of Gylippus, to whom Lysander entrusted bags of gold to take to the city authorities. Those bags were tied at the mouth and then sealed. Gylippus thought that if he cut the bags at the bottom, he could extract some of the coins. Then he could carefully sew the bottom up again, and no one would suspect that gold had been taken because the seals would not be broken. When the bags were opened, to his horror and surprise, there was a note in each bag stating how much it should contain; and so he was detected.

The Word of God has self-verifying clauses in it, so that we cannot run away with a part of it without the remainder of it accusing and convicting us. How will we answer for it "in that day" if we have added to or taken from the Word of the Lord? I am not going to decide for a preacher what he should consider to be the truth of God; but whatever he judges it to be, he should preach it all, and preach it definitely and plainly. If I differ from him, or he from me, we will not differ very much if we are equally honest, straightforward, and God-fearing. The way to peace is not concealment of convictions but the honest expression of them in the power of the Holy Spirit.

One more word. We accept the obligation to preach definitely and distinctly all that is in God's Word. Do not many preach indefinitely, "handling the word of God deceitfully" (2 Cor. 4:2)? You might attend their ministry for years and not know what they believe. I heard that a certain cautious minister was asked by a hearer, "What is your view of the atonement?" He answered, "My dear sir, that is just what I have never told anybody, and you are not going to get it out of me."

This is a strange moral condition for the mind of a preacher of the Gospel. I fear that he is not alone in this reticence. It is said that preachers "consume their own smoke"; that is to say, they keep their doubts for home consumption. Many dare not say in the pulpit what they say secretly at a private meeting of ministers. Is this honest?

I am afraid that some are like the schoolmaster in one of the towns of a southern state in America. A grand old black preacher had taught his people that the world is as flat as a pancake and that the sun goes round it every day. This part of his teaching we do not receive, but some people had done so. Going to the schoolmaster with his boy, one of them asked, "Do you teach the children that the world is round or flat?"

The schoolmaster cautiously answered, "Yes."

The inquirer was puzzled but asked for a clearer answer. "Do you teach your children that the world is round or that the world is flat?"

Then the American schoolmaster answered, "That depends on the opinions of the parents."

I suspect that even in Great Britain, in a few cases, a good deal depends on the leaning of the leading deacon or the principal financial contributor or the gilded youth in the congregation. If it is so, the crime is loathsome.

But whether for this or for any other cause we teach with a double tongue, the result will be highly injurious. I venture here to quote a story that I heard from Mr. Brown, my beloved brother. A beggar called upon a minister to extract money from him. The good man did not like the beggar's appearance much, and he said to him, "I do not care for your case, and I see no special reason why you should come to me."

The beggar replied, "I am sure you would help me if you knew what great benefit I have received from your blessed ministry."

"What is that?" asked the pastor.

The beggar then replied, "Why, sir, when I first came to hear you, I cared neither for God nor the Devil; but now, under your blessed ministry, I have come to love them both."

What marvel if, under some men's shifty talk, people grow to love both truth and falsehood! People will say, "We like this form of doctrine, and we like the other also." The fact is, they would like anything if only a clever deceiver would put it plausibly before them. They admire Moses and Aaron, but they would not say a word against Jannes and Jambres. (See 2 Timothy 3:8.)

We will not join in the confederacy that seems to aim at such a comprehension. We must preach the Gospel so distinctly that our people know what we are preaching. "If the trumpet give an uncertain sound, who shall prepare himself to the battle?" (1 Cor. 14:8). We must not puzzle our people with doubtful speeches.

"Well," said one, "I had a new idea the other day. I did not enlarge upon it, but I just threw it out." That is a very good thing for a preacher to do with most of his new ideas. He should throw them out by all means, but he should mind where he is when he does it. If he throws them out from the pulpit, they may strike somebody and inflict a wound upon faith. He should throw out his fancies, but he should first go alone in a boat a mile out to sea. When he has once thrown out his unconsidered trifles, he should leave them to the fishes.

We have nowadays a class of men who preach Christ and even preach the Gospel, but then they preach a great deal else that is not true. Thus they destroy the good of all that they deliver, and they lure men to error. They want to be called "evangelical" and yet be of the school that is really anti-evangelical.

Look well to these gentlemen. I have heard that a fox, when closely hunted by the dogs, will pretend to be one of them and run with the pack. That is what certain men are aiming at just now; the foxes would pretend to be dogs. But in the case of the fox, his strong scent betrays him, and the dogs soon find him out. Likewise, the scent of false doctrine is not easily concealed, and the game does not work for long.

There are extant ministers of whom we can scarcely tell whether they are dogs or foxes; however, all men will know our quality as long as we live, and they will be in no doubt as to what we believe and teach. In the strongest Saxon words we can find and in the plainest sentences we can put together, we will not hesitate to speak that which we hold as fundamental truth.

Chapter Five

Our Army: The Church

Now we must review our army. What can individual men do in a great crusade? We are associated with all the people of the Lord. We need the members of our churches for comrades; these must go out and win souls for Christ. We need the cooperation of the entire brotherhood and sisterhood. What is to be accomplished unless the saved ones go forth, all of them, for the salvation of others?

A Distinct Church

But the question now is brought up, Is there to be a church at all? Is there to be a distinct army of saints, or are we to include atheists? You have heard of "the church of the future," which we are to have instead of the church of Jesus Christ. All narrowness will cease unless the theaters and the bars should prove too much for the church. Since its extreme will take in atheists, we may hope, in our charity, that it will include evil spirits also. What an astounding church it will be, certainly, when we see it! It will be anything else you like, but not a church. When the soldiers of Christ will have included in their ranks all the bandits of the adversary, will there be any army for Christ at all? Is it not distinctly a capitulation at the very beginning of the war? So I take it to be.

We must not only believe in the church of God, but we must recognize it very distinctly. Some denominations recognize anything and everything more than the church. Such a thing as a meeting of the church is unknown. In some, "the church" signifies the ministers or clergy. It should, however, signify the whole body of the faithful, and there should be an opportunity for these to meet together to act as a church.

It is, I judge, for the church of God to carry on the work of God in the land. The final power and direction is with our Lord Jesus, and under Him it should lie. It should not lie with some few who are chosen by delegation or by patronage, but it should lie with the whole body of believers. We must more and more acknowledge the church that God has committed to our charge. In so doing, we will evoke a strength that otherwise lies dormant. If the church is recognized by Christ Jesus, it is worthy to be recognized by us, for we are the servants of the church.

Yes, we believe that there ought to be a church. But churches are very disappointing things. Every pastor of a large church will admit this in his own soul. I do not know that the churches of today are any worse than they used to be in Paul's time or any better. The churches at Corinth and Laodicea and other cities exhibited grave faults. If there are faults in ours, let us not be amazed; yet let us grieve over such things and labor after a higher standard. Although the members of our churches are not all they ought to be, neither are we ourselves. Yet, if I were to go anywhere for choice company, I would certainly resort to the members of my church.

These are the company I keep:
These are the choicest friends I know.

O Jerusalem, with all your faults, I love you still! The people of God are still the aristocracy of the race; God bless them! Yes, we mean to have a church.

Reality versus Statistics

Now, is that church to be real or statistical? That depends very much on you, dear believers. I would urge you to resolve to have no church unless it is a real one. The fact is that too frequently religious statistics are shockingly false. Cooking of such accounts is not an unknown art in certain places, as we know.

I heard of one case the other day where an increase of four was reported; but had the roll been amended in the least, there must have been a decrease of twenty-five.

Is it not falsehood when numbers are manipulated? There is a way of making figures figure as they should not figure. Never do this. Let us not keep names on our books when they are only names. Many of the good old people like to keep them there and cannot bear to have them removed; but when you do not know where individuals are or who they are, how can you count them? They have gone to America or Australia or to heaven, but as far as your roll is concerned, they are with you still. Is this a right thing? It may not be possible to be absolutely accurate, but let us aim at it.

We ought to look at this in a very serious light and purge ourselves of the vice of false reporting, for God Himself will not bless mere names. It is not His way to work with those who play a false part. If there is not a real person for each name, amend your list. Keep your church real and effective, or make no report. A merely nominal church is a lie. Let it be what it professes to be. We may not glory in statistics; we ought to know the facts.

A Growing Church

Is this church to increase, or is it to die out? It will do either the one or the other. We will see our friends going to heaven, and if there are no young men and young women converted and brought in and added to us, the church on earth will have emigrated to the church triumphant above. What is to be done for the cause and the kingdom of the Master here below?

We should be crying, praying, and pleading that the church may continually grow. We must preach, visit, pray, and labor for this end. May the Lord add unto us "daily such as should be saved" (Acts 2:47)!

If there is no harvest, can the seed be the true seed? Is apostolic doctrine being preached if we never see apostolic results? Oh, my brothers, our hearts should be ready to break if there is no increase in our flocks. O Lord, we beseech You, send prosperity now!

A Praying Church

If a church is to be what it ought to be for the purposes of God, it must be trained in the holy art of prayer. Churches without prayer meetings are grievously common. Even if there were only one such as that, it would be one to weep over. In many churches, the prayer meeting is only the skeleton of a gathering: the form is kept up, but the people do not come. There is no interest and no power in connection with the meeting.

Let it not be so with you! Continually meet together for prayer. Rouse yourselves to incessant supplication. There is a holy art in it. "Study to show [yourselves] approved unto God" (2 Tim. 2:15) by your prayerfulness. If you pray yourself, you will want others to pray with you. When they begin to pray with you and for you and for the work of the

Lord, they will want more prayer themselves, and the appetite will grow.

Believe me, if a church does not pray, it is dead. Instead of putting united prayer last, put it first. Everything will hinge on the power of prayer in the church.

A Busy Church

We ought to have all of the people in our churches busy for God. What is the use of a church that simply assembles to hear sermons, even as a family gathers to eat its meals? What, I say, is the profit if it does no work? Are not many professors of Christ sadly indolent in the Lord's work, though diligent enough in their own?

Because of Christian idleness, we hear of the necessity for amusements, and we hear all sorts of nonsense. If they were at work for the Lord Jesus, we should not hear of this. A good woman said to a housewife, "Mrs. So-and-so, how do you manage to entertain yourself?"

"Why," she replied, "my dear, you see there are so many children that there is much work to be done in my house."

"Yes," said the other, "I see it. I see that there is much work to be done in your house; but since it is never done, I was wondering how you entertained yourself."

Much needs to be done by a Christian church within its own congregation, for the neighborhood, for the poor and the fallen, for the heathen world, and so forth. If this work is well attended to, minds, hearts, hands, and tongues will be occupied, and diversions will not be asked for. Let idleness come in, along with the spirit that rules lazy people, and there will arise a desire to be amused. What amusements they are, too! If religion is not a farce with some congregations, at any rate, more of them turn out to see a farce than to unite in prayer. I cannot understand it.

The man who is all aglow with love for Jesus finds little need for amusement. He has no time for trifling. He is in dead earnest to save souls, establish the truth, and enlarge the kingdom of his Lord.

There has always been some pressing claim for the cause of God upon me; when that is settled, there has been another and another and another. The scramble has been to find opportunity to do the work that must be done, and hence I have not had the time for roaming abroad after frivolities.

Oh, to have a working church! The German churches, when our dear friend, Mr. Oncken, was alive, always carried out the rule of asking every member, "What are you going to do for Christ?" and they put the answer down in a book. The one thing that was required of every member was that he should continue doing something for the Savior. If he ceased to do anything, it was a matter for church discipline; for he had become an idle professor of Christ, and he could not be allowed to remain in the church like a drone in a hive of working bees. He must do or go.

Oh, for a vineyard without a barren fig tree! At present, most of our sacred

warfare is carried on by a small body of
intensely living, earnest people, and the
rest are either in the hospital or are
mere camp followers. We are thankful
for that consecrated few, but we long to
see the altar fire consuming all that is
professedly laid upon the altar.

An All-Saints Church

Brothers, we want churches also
that produce saints—men of mighty
faith and prevailing prayer, men of holy
living and of consecrated giving, men
filled with the Holy Spirit. We must
have these saints as rich clusters, or
surely we are not branches of the True
Vine.

I would desire to see in every church
a Mary sitting at Jesus' feet, a Martha
serving Jesus, a Peter and a John; but
the best name for a church is "All
Saints." All believers should be saints,
and all may be saints. We have no connection with "the Latter-day Saints,"
but we love everyday saints. Oh, for
more of them!

If God will so help us that the whole company of the faithful will, each one of them individually, come to the fullness of the stature of a man in Christ Jesus (Eph. 4:13), then we will see greater things than these. Glorious times will come when believers have glorious characters.

A Knowledgeable Church

We also want churches that know the truth and are well taught in the things of God. What do some Christian people know? They come and hear the preacher instruct them with the plenitude of his wisdom, but how little they receive to lay by in store for edification! The fault lies partly with the preacher and partly with the listener. If the preacher would teach better, the listener would learn better.

See how little many professing Christians know—not enough to give them discernment between living truth and deadly error. Old-fashioned believers could give you chapter and verse for what they believed, but how few of such remain! Our venerable forefathers were at home when conversing about the covenants. I love men who love the covenant of grace and base their divinity on it; the doctrine of the covenants is the key of theology.

They that feared the Lord spoke often to one another. They used to speak of everlasting life and all that comes with it. They had a good argument for this belief and an excellent reason for that other doctrine. To try to shake them was by no means a hopeful task; you might as well have hoped to shake the pillars of the universe. They were steadfast and could not be carried about "with every wind of doctrine" (Eph. 4:14). They knew what they knew, and they held fast to what they had learned.

What is to become of our country with the present deluge of Romanism pouring upon us through the ritualistic party, unless our churches abound in firm believers who can discern between the regeneration of the Holy Spirit and its ceremonial substitute? What is to come of our churches in this day of skepticism, when every fixed truth is pointed at with the finger of doubt, unless our people have the truths of the Gospel written in their hearts? Oh, for a church of out-and-out believers, impervious to the soul-destroying doubt that pours upon us in showers!

A Missionary Church

Yet, all this would not reach our ideal. We want a church of a missionary character that will go forth to gather out a people unto God from all parts of the world. A church is a soul-saving company, or it is nothing. If the salt exercises no preserving influence on that which surrounds it, what is the use of it? (See Matthew 5:13.)

Some shrink from effort in their immediate neighborhoods because of the poverty and vice of the people. I remember a minister who is now deceased; a very good man he was, too, in many respects. However, he utterly amazed me by a reply that he made to a question of mine. I remarked that he had an awful neighborhood around his chapel, and I said, "Are you able to do much for them?"

He answered, "No, I feel almost glad that we keep clear of them. You see, if any of them were converted, it would be a terrible burden on us." I knew him to be the soul of caution and prudence, but this took me aback. I then sought an explanation. "Well," he said, "we would have to support them. They are mostly thieves and harlots. If converted, they would have no means of livelihood, and we are a poor people and could not support them!"

He was a devout man and one with whom it was profitable to converse, and yet that was how he had gradually come to look at the case. His people could barely sustain the expenses of worship, and so cold penury repressed a gracious zeal and froze the genial current of his soul. There was a great deal of common sense in what he said, but yet it was an awful thing to be able to say it.

We want a people who will not forever sing:

We are a garden walled around,
    Chosen and made peculiar ground;
A little spot enclosed by grace,
    Out of the world's wild wilderness.

It is a good verse for occasional singing, but not when it comes to mean, "We are very few, and we want to be." No, no, brothers! We are a little detachment of the King's soldiers detained in a foreign country on garrison duty, yet we mean not only to hold the fort but to add territory to our Lord's dominion. We are not to be driven out; on the contrary, we are going to drive out the Canaanites. This land belongs to us—it is given to us by the Lord—and we will subdue it. May we be fired with the spirit of discoverers and conquerors, and may we never rest while there yet remains a class to be rescued, a region to be evangelized!

We are rowing like lifeboat men upon a stormy sea, and we are hurrying to yonder wreck where men are perishing. If we cannot draw that old wreck to shore, we will at least, by the power of God, rescue the perishing, save life, and bear the redeemed to the shores of salvation. Our mission, like our Lord's, is to gather out the chosen of God from among men, that they may live to the glory of God.

Every saved man should be, under God, a savior; and the church is not in a right state until she has reached that conception of herself. The elect church is saved that she may save, cleansed that she may cleanse, blessed that she may bless. All the world is the field, and all the members of the church should work in the field for the great Husbandman. Waste lands are to be reclaimed, and forests broken up by the plow, until "the solitary place" begins to "blossom as the rose" (Isa. 35:1). We must not be content with holding our own; we must invade the territories of the Prince of Darkness.

Servants of the Church

What is our relation to this church? What is our position in it? We are servants. May we always know our place and keep it! The highest place in the church will always come to the man

who willingly chooses the lowest, while
he who aspires to be great among his
brothers will sink to be least of all. (See
Matthew 20:26–27; Mark 9:35; 10:44.)

Certain men might have been something if they had not thought themselves so. A consciously great man is an
evidently little one. A lord over God's
heritage is a base usurper.

He who in his heart and soul is always ready to serve the very least of the
family, who expects to be imposed
upon, and who willingly sacrifices reputation and friendship for Christ's sake,
will fulfill a heaven-sent ministry. We
are sent "not to be ministered unto, but
to minister" (Matt. 20:28).

Let us sing unto our Well-Beloved:

There's not a lamb in all thy flock,
I would disdain to feed;
There's not a foe before whose face
I'd fear thy cause to plead.

Examples to the Church

We must also be examples to the
flock. He that cannot be safely imitated

ought not to be tolerated in a pulpit. Did I hear of a minister who was always disputing for preeminence? Or of another who was mean and covetous? Or of a third whose conversation was not always chaste? Or of a fourth who did not rise, as a rule, until eleven o'clock in the morning? I would hope that this last rumor was altogether false. An idle minister—what will become of him? A pastor who neglects his office? Does he expect to go to heaven? I was about to say, "If he does go there at all, may it be soon." A lazy minister is a creature despised of men and abhorred of God.

"You give your minister such a small salary," I said to a farmer. "Why, the poor man cannot live on it."

The answer was, "Look here, sir! I tell you what: we give him a good deal more than he earns." It is a sad pity when that can be said; it is an injury to all those who follow our sacred calling.

We are to be examples to the flock in all things. In all diligence, in all gentleness, in all humility, and in all holiness, we are to excel. When Caesar went on his wars, one thing always helped his soldiers to bear hardships: they knew that Caesar fared as they fared. He marched if they marched, he thirsted if they thirsted, and he was always in the heat of the battle if they were fighting.

We must do more than others if we are officers in Christ's army. We must not cry, "Go on," but, "Come on." People may justly expect of us, at the very least, that we will be among the most self-denying, the most laborious, and the most earnest in the church, and somewhat more. We cannot expect to see holy churches if we who are obligated to be their examples are unsanctified. If any of our congregation have consecration and sanctification that is evident to all men, God has blessed them, and God will bless them more and more. If these are lacking in us, we need not search far to find the cause of our nonsuccess.

My next topic, the Holy Spirit, is the most important topic of this book. Here allow me to pray for His help, whose name and person I would

magnify. Come, Holy Spirit, heavenly
Dove, and rest upon us now!

Chapter Six

Our Strength:
The Holy Spirit

Granted that we preach the Word alone; granted that we are surrounded by a model church, which unfortunately is not always the case; but granted that it is so, our strength is the next consideration. This must come from the Spirit of God. We believe in the Holy Spirit and in our absolute dependence upon Him. We believe, but do we believe practically? As to ourselves and our own work, do we believe in the Holy Spirit? Do we believe because we habitually prove the truth of the doctrine?

We must depend on the Spirit in our preparations. Is this the fact with us all? Are you in the habit of working your way into the meaning of texts by the guidance of the Holy Spirit? Every man that goes to the land of heavenly knowledge must work his passage there. But, he must work out his passage in the strength of the Holy Spirit, or he will arrive at some island in the sea of fancy and never set his foot on the sacred shores of the truth.

You do not know the truth because you have read *Hodge's Outlines, Fuller's Gospel Worthy of all Acceptation, Owen on the Spirit,* or any other classic of our faith. You do not know the truth merely because you accept the Westminster Assembly's Confession and have studied it perfectly. No, we know nothing until we are taught by the Holy Spirit, who speaks to the heart rather than to the ear.

It is an amazing fact that we do not even hear the voice of Jesus until the Spirit rests upon us. John says, "I was in the Spirit on the Lord's day, and heard behind me a great voice" (Rev. 1:10). He did not hear that voice until he was in the Spirit. How many heavenly words we miss because we do not abide in the Spirit!

We cannot succeed in supplication unless the Holy Spirit helps our infirmities, for true prayer is "praying in the Holy Ghost" (Jude 1:20). The Spirit makes an atmosphere around every living prayer; within that circle, prayer lives and prevails; outside of it, prayer is a dead formality. As to ourselves, then, in our study, in prayer, in thought, in word, and in deed, we must depend on the Holy Spirit.

In the pulpit do we really and truly rest upon the aid of the Spirit? I do not censure anyone for his mode of preaching. However, I must confess that it seems very odd to me when someone prays that the Holy Spirit will help him in preaching, and then I see him put his hand behind him and take a manuscript out of his pocket, so fashioned that he can place it in the middle of his Bible and read from it without being suspected of doing so. These precautions for ensuring secrecy look as though the man was a little ashamed of his paper, but I think he should be far more ashamed of his precautions.

Does he expect the Spirit of God to bless him while he is practicing a trick? And how can He help him when he reads from a paper from which anyone else might read without the Spirit's aid? What does the Holy Spirit have to do with the business? Truly, He may have had something to do with the manuscript in the composing of it, but in the pulpit His aid is superfluous. The truer thing would be to thank the Holy Spirit for assistance rendered and ask that what He has enabled us to get into our pockets may now enter the people's hearts.

Still, if the Holy Spirit should have anything to say to the people that is not in the paper, how can He say it by us? He seems to me to be very effectually blocked as to freshness of utterance by that method of ministry. Still, it is not for me to censure, although I may quietly plead for liberty in prophesying and room for the Lord to give us in the same hour what we should speak. (See Matthew 10:19.)

Furthermore, we must depend on the Spirit of God for our results. No man among us really thinks that he could regenerate a soul. We are not so foolish as to claim power to change a heart of stone. We do not dare to presume quite so much, and yet we may come to think that, by our experience, we can help people over spiritual difficulties. Can we? We may be hopeful that our enthusiasm will drive the living church before us and drag the dead world after us. Will it be so? Perhaps we imagine that if we could only get up a revival, we would easily secure large additions to the church? Is it worthwhile to get up a revival? Are not all true revivals to be got down? We may persuade ourselves that drums and trumpets and shouting will do a great deal. But "the LORD [is] not in the wind" (1 Kings 19:11).

Results worth having come from that silent but omnipotent Worker whose name is the Spirit of God. We must trust in Him, and in Him only, for the conversion of a single Sunday-school child and for every genuine revival. To keep the people together and to build them up into a holy temple, we must look to Him. The Spirit might say, even as our Lord did, "Without me ye can do nothing" (John 15:5).

What is God's church without the Holy Spirit? Ask what would Hermon be without its dew (see Psalm 133:3), or Egypt without its Nile. Behold the land of Canaan when the curse of Elijah fell upon it, and for three years it felt neither dew nor rain. Such would Christendom become without the Spirit. Valleys without their brooks, cities without their wells, cornfields without the sun, or the vintage without the summer—that is what our churches would be without the Spirit. You may as well think of day without light, life without breath, or heaven without God as of Christian service without the Holy Spirit. Nothing can supply His place if He is absent; the pastures are a desert, the fruitful fields are a wilderness, Sharon languishes, and Carmel is burned with fire.

Blessed Spirit of the Lord, forgive us for being so despiteful to You by our forgetfulness of You, by our proud self-sufficiency, by resisting Your influences, and by quenching Your fire! Henceforth, work in us according to Your own excellence. Make our hearts tenderly impressible, then turn us as wax to the seal, and stamp upon us the image of the Son of God.

With some such prayer and confession of faith as this, let us pursue our subject in the power of the good Spirit of whom we speak.

What does the Holy Spirit do? Beloved, what is there of good work that He does not do? It is His to quicken, to convince, to illuminate, to cleanse, to guide, to preserve, to console, to confirm, to perfect, and to use. How much might be said under each one of these headings! It is He that works in us "to will and to do" (Phil. 2:13). He that has done all things is God. Glory be unto the

Holy Spirit for all that He has accomplished in such poor, imperfect natures as ours!

We can do nothing apart from the life-sap that flows to us from Jesus the Vine. That which is our own is fit only to cause us shame and embarrassment. We never go a step towards heaven without the Holy Spirit. We never lead another on the heavenward road without the Holy Spirit. We have no acceptable thought, word, or deed apart from the Holy Spirit. Even the uplifting of the eye of hope or the intense prayer of the heart's desire must be His work. All good things are of Him and through Him, from beginning to end. There is no fear of exaggerating here. Do we, however, translate this conviction into our actual practice?

Instead of expounding on what the Spirit of God does, let me refer to your experience and ask you a question or two. Do you remember times when the Spirit of God has been graciously present in fullness of power with you and with your church? What seasons those have been! That Sabbath was a grand day. Those services were like the worship of Jacob when he said, "Surely the LORD is in this place!" (Gen. 28:16).

What mutual communicating goes on between the preacher in the Spirit and the people in the Spirit! The people's eyes seem to talk as much as the preacher's tongue. They are then a very different people from what they are on common occasions. There is even a beauty upon their faces while they are glorifying the Lord Jesus, and they are enjoying and drinking in the teaching.

Have you ever seen a gentleman of the modern school enjoying his own preaching? Our evangelical preachers are very happy in delivering what our liberal friends are pleased to call their "platitudes," but the moderns in their wisdom feel no such joy. Can you imagine a Downgrader in the glow that our Welsh friends call the *Hwyl*? How grimly they comment on the post-exilic theory! They remind me of Ruskin's expression: "Turner had no joy of his mill." I grant you that there is nothing to enjoy, and they are evidently glad to get through their task of piling up meatless bones. They stand at an empty manger, amusing themselves by biting their crib. They get through their preaching, and they are dull enough until Monday comes with a football match or an entertainment in the schoolroom or a political meeting. To them, preaching is work, though they do not put much work into it.

The old preachers, and some of those who are young but are said to be obsolete, think the pulpit a throne or a triumphal chariot; they are near heaven when helped to preach with power. Poor fools that we are, preaching our "antiquated" Gospel! We do enjoy the task. Our gloomy doctrines make us very happy. Strange, is it not? The Gospel is evidently marrow and fatness to us. Our beliefs—although, of course, they are very absurd and unphilosophical—do content us and make us very confident and happy. I may say about some of my brothers that their very eyes seem to sparkle and their souls seem to glow, while they are enlarging on free grace and dying love.

When we have the presence of God, then we and our hearers are carried away with heavenly delight. That is not all. When the Spirit of God is present, every saint loves his fellow saint, and there is no strife among us unless it is about who will be the most loving. Then prayer is wrestling and prevailing, and ministry is sowing good seed and reaping large sheaves. Then conversions are plentiful, restorations are abundant, and advances in grace are seen on every side. Hallelujah! With the Spirit of God, all goes well.

But do you know the opposite condition? I hope you do not. It is death in life. I trust you have never been cruel enough in your scientific experiments to put a mouse under an air pump and gradually exhaust the receiver. I have read of the fatal experiment. Alas, poor mouse! As the air gets thinner and thinner, how great are his sufferings; and when it is all gone, there he lies—dead.

Have you ever been under an exhausted receiver, spiritually? You have only been there long enough to perceive that the sooner you escaped, the better for you.

Said one to me the other day, "Well, about the sermon that I heard from the modern theologian, there was no great harm in it, for on this occasion he kept clear of false doctrine. However, the whole affair was so intensely cold. I felt like a man who has fallen down a crevice in a glacier; I felt shut in as if I could not breathe the air of heaven."

You know that arctic cold. It may occasionally be felt even where the doctrine is sound. When the Spirit of God is gone, even truth itself becomes an iceberg. How wretched is frozen and lifeless religion! The Holy Spirit has gone, and all energy and enthusiasm have gone with Him. The scene becomes like that described in the "Ancient Mariner" when the ship was becalmed:

The very deep did rot,
Alas, that ever this should be!

Yea, slimy things did crawl with legs
Upon the slimy sea.

Within the ship all was death. And
we have seen it so within a church. I am
tempted to apply Coleridge's lines to
many aspects of those churches that de-
serve the name "congregations of the
dead." He describes how the bodies of
the dead were inspired and the ship
moved on, each dead man fulfilling his
office in a dead and formal fashion:

The helmsman steered, the ship
    moved on;
Yet never a breeze up blew;
The mariners all 'gan work the ropes,
Where they were wont to do;
They raised their limbs like lifeless
    tools—
We were a ghastly crew.

All living fellowship was lacking, for
the Ancient Mariner said:

The body of my brother's son
Stood by me, knee to knee:

113

> The body and I pulled at one rope,
> But he said nought to me.

It is much the same in those "respectable" congregations where no man knows his fellow, and a dignified isolation replaces all saintly communion. To the preacher, if he is the only living man in the company, the church affords very dreary society. His sermons fall on ears that do not hear them right.

> 'Twas night, calm night, the moon
>   was high;
> The dead men stood together.
> All stood together on the deck
> For a charnel-dungeon fitter:
> All fixed on me their stony eyes,
> That in the moon did glitter.

Yes, the preacher's moonlight, cold and cheerless, falls on faces that are like it. The discourse impresses their emotionless intellects and fixes their stony eyes. But hearts? Well, hearts are not in fashion in those regions. Hearts are for the realm of life, but without the Holy Spirit, what do congregations know of true life? If the Holy Spirit has gone, death reigns, and the church is a tomb. Therefore, we must entreat Him to abide with us, and we must never rest until He does so. O believers, let it not be that I talk to you about this and that then we permit the matter to drop, but let us each one with heart and soul seek to have the power of the Holy Spirit abiding upon him.

Have we received the Holy Spirit? Is He with us now? If it is so, how can we secure His future presence? How can we constrain Him to abide with us?

I would say, first, treat Him as He should be treated. Worship Him as the adorable Lord God. Never call the Holy Spirit "it," nor speak of Him as if He were a doctrine, or an influence, or an orthodox myth. Reverence Him, love Him, and trust Him with familiar yet reverent confidence. He is God; let Him be God to you.

See to it that you act in conformity with His working. The sailor to the East cannot create the winds at his pleasure. However, he knows when the trade winds blow, and he takes advantage of the season to speed his vessel. Put out to sea in holy enterprise when the heavenly wind is with you. Take the sacred tide at its flood. Meetings should be increased when you feel that the Spirit of God is blessing them. The truth should be pressed home more earnestly than ever when the Lord is opening ears and hearts to accept it. You will soon know when there is dew about; prize the gracious visitation.

The farmer says, "Make hay while the sun shines." You cannot make the sun shine; that is quite out of your power. But you can use the sun while it shines. "When thou hearest the sound of a going in the tops of the mulberry trees, that then thou shalt bestir thyself" (2 Sam. 5:24). Be diligent in season and out of season (2 Tim. 4:2), but in a lively season be doubly laborious.

Evermore, in beginning, in continuing, and in ending any and every good work, consciously and in truth depend upon the Holy Spirit. Even a sense of your need of Him He must give you, and the prayers with which you entreat Him to come must come from Him. You are engaged in a work so spiritual, so far above all human power, that to forget the Spirit is to ensure defeat. Recognize the Holy Spirit as absolutely indispensable in your efforts, and go so far as to say to Him, "If thy presence go not with [me], carry us not up hence" (Exod. 33:15).

Rest only in Him and then reserve for Him all the glory. Be especially mindful of this, for this is a tender point with Him: He will not give His glory to another. Take care to praise the Spirit of God from your inmost heart, and gratefully wonder that He should condescend to work through you. Please Him by glorifying Christ. Render Him homage by yielding yourself to His impulses and by hating everything that grieves Him. The consecration of your whole being will be the best psalm in His praise.

There are a few things that I would have you remember, and then I will be done. Remember that the Holy Spirit has His ways and methods, and there

are some things that He will not do.
Remember that He makes no promise to
bless compromises. If we make a treaty
with error or sin, we do it at our own
risk. If we do anything that we are not
clear about, if we tamper with truth or
holiness, if we are friends of the world, if
we make provision for the flesh, if we
preach halfheartedly and are allied with
those in error, we have no promise that
the Holy Spirit will go with us.

The great promise runs in quite another strain:

> *Wherefore come out from among*
> *them, and be ye separate, saith the*
> *Lord, and touch not the unclean*
> *thing; and I will receive you, And*
> *will be a Father unto you, and ye*
> *shall be my sons and daughters,*
> *saith the Lord Almighty.*
>
> *(2 Cor. 6:17–18)*

Only in that one place in the New Testament, with the exception of the book
of Revelation, is God called by the name
of "the Lord God Almighty." If you want
to know what great things the Lord can

do as the Lord God Almighty, be separate from the world and from those who apostatize from the truth.

The title "Lord God Almighty" is evidently quoted from the Old Testament: "El-Shaddai," God all-sufficient, the God who nurtures and provides. We will never know the utmost power of God for supplying all our needs until we have cut connection once for all with everything that is not according to His mind. It was grand of Abraham when he said to the king of Sodom, "I will not take from you"—a Babylonian garment or a wedge of gold? No, no. He said, "I will not take from a thread even to a shoelatchet" (Gen. 14:23). That was a clear-cut separation. The man of God will have nothing to do with Sodom or with false doctrine. If you see anything that is evil, cut yourself off from it. Be done with those who are done with truth. Then you will be prepared to receive the promise, and not until then.

Dear believers, remember that wherever there is great love, there is sure to be great jealousy. "Love is strong as death" (Song 8:6). What next? "Jealousy is cruel as the grave" (Song 8:6). "God is love" (1 John 4:8), and for that very reason "the LORD thy God is a jealous God" (Deut. 6:15). Keep clear of everything that defiles or that grieves the Holy Spirit. If He is vexed with us, we will soon be put to shame before the enemy.

Note, next, that He makes no promise to cowardice. If you allow the fear of man to rule you and wish to save self from suffering or ridicule, you will find small comfort in the promise of God. "Whosoever will save his life shall lose it" (Matt. 16:25). The promises of the Holy Spirit to us in our warfare are to those who conduct themselves like men and are made brave by faith in the hour of conflict. I wish that we would come to this pass, that we utterly despised ridicule and slander.

Oh, to have the self-oblivion of that Italian martyr of whom Foxe speaks! They condemned him to be burned alive, and he heard the sentence calmly. But, you know, no matter how delightful it is to burn martyrs, it is also expensive. The mayor of the town did not care to pay for the wood, and the priests who had accused him also wished to do the work without personal expense. So they had an angry squabble, and there stood the poor man for whose benefit this kindling was to be contributed, quietly hearing their mutual recriminations. Finding that they could not settle it, he said, "Gentlemen, I will end your dispute. It is a pity that you should, either of you, be at so much expense to find sticks for my burning; and, for my Lord's sake, I will even pay for the wood that burns me, if you please."

There is a fine touch of scorn as well as meekness there. I do not know that I would have paid that bill, but I have even felt inclined to go a little out of the way to help the enemies of the truth to find fuel for their criticisms of me. Yes, yes, I will yet be more vile and give them more to complain of. I will go through with the controversy for Christ's sake and do nothing whatsoever to quiet their wrath.

121

Fellow believers, if you trim a little, if you try to save a little of your reputation with the men of the apostasy, it will go ill with you. He that is ashamed of Christ and His Word in this evil generation will find that Christ is ashamed of him at the last. (See Mark 8:38.)

I will be very brief on these points. Remember, next, that the Holy Spirit will never set his seal to falsehood. Never! If we do not preach the truth, God will not own it. Look well to this.

What is more, the Holy Spirit never puts His signature on a blank page. That would be unwise on the part of man, and the Holy Lord will not perpetrate such a folly. If we do not speak clear doctrine with plainness of speech, the Holy Spirit will not put His signature to our empty prating. If we do not come out distinctly with "Christ, and him crucified" (1 Cor. 2:2), we may say farewell to true success.

Next, remember that the Holy Spirit will never sanction sin. To bless the ministry of some men would be to sanction their evil ways. "Be ye clean, that bear the vessels of the LORD" (Isa. 52:11). Let your character correspond with your teaching, and let your churches be purged from open transgressors, lest the Holy Spirit disown your teaching, not for its own sake, but because of the bad smell of unholy living that dishonors it.

Remember, also, that He will never encourage idleness. The Holy Spirit will not come in to rescue the speaker from the consequences of willful neglect of the Word of God and study. If we allow ourselves to go up and down the whole week doing nothing, we may not climb the pulpit stairs and dream that the Lord will there and then tell us what to speak. If help were promised to such, then the lazier the man, the better the sermon. If the Holy Spirit worked only by impromptu speakers, the less we read our Bibles and the less we meditated on them the better. If it were wrong to quote from books, attention to reading would not have been commanded. All this is obviously absurd, and you should not fall into such a delusion.

Those who preach God's Word are obligated to be much in meditation and give themselves wholly to the Word of God and prayer (Acts 6:4). When we have minded these things, we may look for the Spirit's approval and cooperation. We ought to prepare the sermon as if all depended on us; then we are to trust the Spirit of God, knowing that all depends on Him. The Holy Spirit sends no one into the harvest to sleep among the sheaves but to bear "the burden and heat of the day" (Matt. 20:12). We may well pray to God to send more laborers into the vineyard (Luke 10:2); for the Spirit will be with the strength of laborers, but He will not be the friend of loiterers.

Recollect, too, that the Holy Spirit will not bless us in order to sustain our pride. Is it not possible that we may be wishing for a great blessing that we may be thought great men? This will hinder our success; the string of the bow is out of place, and the arrow will veer aside. What does God do with men that are proud? Does He exalt them? I think not.

Herod made an eloquent oration, and he put on a dazzling, silver robe that glistened in the sun. When the people saw his garments and listened to his charming voice, they cried, "It is the voice of a god, and not of a man" (Acts 12:22); but the Lord smote him, and he was eaten by worms.

Worms have a prescriptive right to proud flesh; when we get very mighty and very big, the worms expect to make a meal of us. "Pride goeth before destruction, and an haughty spirit before a fall" (Prov. 16:18). Keep humble if you want the Spirit of God with you. The Holy Spirit takes no pleasure in the inflated oratory of the proud; how can He? Would you have Him sanction bombast? "Walk humbly with thy God" (Mic. 6:8), for you cannot walk with Him in any other way; and if you do not walk with Him, your walking will be vain.

Consider, also, that the Holy Spirit will not dwell where there is strife. Let us "follow peace with all men" (Heb. 12:14), and especially let us keep peace in our churches. Some of you are not yet favored with this blessing, and possibly it is not your fault. You may have inherited old feuds. In many a small community, all the members of the congregation are cousins to one another, and relations usually agree to disagree. When cousins cozen their cousins, the seeds of ill will are sown, and these intrude even into church life.

The former preacher's high-handedness in past time may have bred a good deal of quarreling for many years to come. He was a man of war from his youth, and even when he is gone, the spirits that he called from the vast deep remain to haunt the spot. I fear you cannot expect much blessing, for the Holy Dove does not dwell by troubled waters; He chooses to come where brotherly love continues. For great principles and matters of holy discipline, we may risk peace itself, but for self or party may such conduct be far from us.

Lastly, remember the Holy Spirit will only bless in conformity with His own set purpose. Our Lord explains what that purpose is: "He shall glorify me" (John 16:14). He has come forth for this grand end, and He will not put up with anything short of it. If, then, we do not preach Christ, what is the Holy Spirit to do with our preaching? If we do not make the Lord Jesus glorious, if we do not lift Him high in the esteem of men, if we do not labor to make Him King of Kings and Lord of Lords, we will not have the Holy Spirit with us. Vain will be rhetoric, music, architecture, energy, and social status; if our one design is not to magnify the Lord Jesus, we will work alone and work in vain.

This is all that I have to say to you at this time, but it is a great all if first considered and then carried out. May it have practical effect upon us! It will if the great Worker uses it, and not otherwise.

Go forth, O soldiers of Jesus, with "the sword of the Spirit, which is the word of God" (Eph. 6:17). Go forth with the companies of the godly whom you lead, and let every man "be strong in the Lord, and in the power of his might" (Eph. 6:10). As men "alive from the dead" (Rom. 6:13), go forth in the quickening power of the Holy Spirit; you have no other strength.

May the blessing of the Triune God rest upon you, one and all, for the Lord Jesus Christ's sake! Amen.